King Charles III

A Little Golden Book® Biography

By Jen Arena

Illustrated by Monique Dong

A GOLDEN BOOK • NEW YORK

Text copyright © 2023 by Jen Arena
Cover and interior illustrations copyright © 2023 by Monique Dong
All rights reserved. Published in the United States by Golden Books, an imprint of
Random House Children's Books, a division of Penguin Random House LLC, 1745 Broadway,
New York, NY 10019. Golden Books, A Golden Book, A Little Golden Book, the G colophon,
and the distinctive gold spine are registered trademarks of Penguin Random House LLC.
rhcbooks.com
Educators and librarians, for a variety of teaching tools, visit us at RHTeachersLibrarians.com
Library of Congress Control Number: 2022949673
ISBN 978-0-593-70643-5 (trade) — ISBN 978-0-593-70644-2 (ebook)
Printed in the United States of America
10 9 8 7 6 5 4 3 2 1

Charles III waited his whole life to be king.

On November 14, 1948, Charles Philip Arthur George was born in Buckingham Palace in London, England. His mother, Elizabeth, was a princess. His grandfather, George VI, was king of the United Kingdom.

Just hours after being born, baby Charles was whisked away to the ballroom. The people in the palace wanted to see the new prince!

When he was three years old, his mother became queen. That made Charles, Queen Elizabeth II's oldest child, next in line for the throne. One day, he would be king.

Charles's parents were very busy. Still, his mother taught him to ride horses. His father, Prince Philip, taught him to fish. Mostly, though, his grandmother and nanny raised him.

Charles loved being outside. He learned
the names of trees and wildflowers. He played
games with his little sister, Anne, and spent time
at his grandmother's house. He fed cows, climbed
hay bales, and watched pigs.

As a boy, Charles was shy, thoughtful, and a little awkward. He was sick a lot. People teased him because his ears stuck out. Worried he wasn't tough enough, his father sent him away to school—first to a private school in the country and then, at age thirteen, to Gordonstoun in a far-off part of Scotland. Philip thought it would build character. After all, it was the same school he had gone to.

Students had to sleep with the windows open, even in winter. Some boys woke up with snow on their beds! Every morning, they ran a mile before breakfast. The showers were cold. The school served lots of boiled potatoes for lunch and dinner. Worst of all, bullies picked on the young prince.

Charles hated it there. But he toughed it out.

In 1969, Queen Elizabeth kept a promise from years earlier and made Charles the Prince of Wales. To prepare, he stayed in Wales for ten weeks, studying Welsh culture and history.

Five hundred million people around the world watched on TV as he knelt on a red pillow. His mother placed a crown on his head. He gave a speech, part of it in Welsh.

Charles looked like a king that day. How long would he have to wait to *be* king?

Charles got his college degree and served
in the Royal Air Force and the Royal Navy.
He learned to fly jets and helicopters and
commanded a type of ship called a minesweeper.

He competed in a lot of polo matches, a sport played on horseback. He skied. He windsurfed. He drove a sports car. Some newspapers called him "Action Man." But Charles enjoyed quieter hobbies, too, like reading, fishing, dancing, and painting.

Charles liked having fun, but he also wanted to make a difference. He started a charity with money he earned from serving in the navy. The Prince's Trust helped troubled young people, teaching them skills to get good jobs.

Over the years, Charles built the Prince's Trust into a powerful force. He convinced rock stars to play benefit concerts. He raised money from movie stars.

At the same time, his work for the royal family kept him on the move. He met presidents and prime ministers. He traveled all over the world.

People began asking: Would Prince Charles ever settle down and get married?

When he was thirty-two years old, Charles asked Diana Spencer to marry him. She was thirteen years younger than him. They hadn't dated long and didn't know each other well, but she was very pretty and came from a good family.

Their wedding was like a fairy tale. Charles wore his Royal Navy uniform. Diana wore a beautiful gown. They rode in a horse-drawn carriage.

Soon Diana gave birth to a son, William. As Charles's first child, one day, William would be king after his father. Two years later, a second son, Harry, was born.

Charles and Diana didn't have a happy
marriage. Charles liked the countryside. Diana
loved London and city life. Charles relaxed
around a small circle of friends and family. Diana
lit up around new people.

Ever since he was a baby, people had flocked
to see Prince Charles. Now Diana got more
attention than he did!

They spent more and more time apart. Charles shared his love of nature with William and Harry. He built them a tree house with a thatched roof. Their mum took them to movie theaters and amusement parks.

Several years later, Charles and Diana got a divorce.

Meanwhile, Charles found his own path as
a royal. His mother, the Queen, kept her opinions
to herself. Charles didn't.

He warned the public about global warming. He
urged farmers to return to simpler methods and
avoid using chemicals on their crops. He showed
them how by turning his private home into an
organic farm.

He spoke out against modern architecture. Instead, he planned his ideal village and started its construction. Poundbury had lots of green space, winding streets, small houses, shops, and town squares. Some of the houses went to people without much money. Charles called Poundbury the project of his lifetime.

Then tragedy struck the family. Princess
Diana died in a car accident in Paris. Charles
felt the loss deeply for his sons.

William, fifteen, and Harry, twelve, honored
their mother by walking the one-mile funeral
route in front of thousands of people mourning
their favorite princess. Charles, his father,
Philip, and their uncle walked alongside them.

In 2005, older and wiser, Prince Charles married again. He and Camilla Parker Bowles had been friends for many years.

This time, the marriage was a happy one.

Prince Charles watched his sons grow up, marry, and have children of their own. As the Queen got older, Charles took over more of his mother's duties. She passed away after a very long and full life, having served as queen for seventy years.

Charles was three years old when his mother became queen. At seventy-three, he was the oldest person in British history to take the throne. On May 6, 2023, he was crowned king of England.

After waiting a lifetime, Prince Charles became King Charles III.